Exhibit B

by

Brendan Hawthorne

Cover Photographs by Lynn Hawthorne

Illustrated by Tina Keevil

Image production by Dr Varney

THE KATES HILL PRESS

First Published By THE KATES HILL PRESS
24 Fernhurst Drive, Brierley Hill, DY5 4PU

ISBN: 978 1 904552 38 3

British Library CIP Data:
A catalogue record for this book is available
from the British Library

Printed By: Lightning Source UK Ltd, Milton Keynes

Cover Design By: © Brendan Hawthorne
Cover Photograph By: © Lynn Hawthorne
Illustrations By: © Tina Keevil

Exhibit B

(A Gallery of Virtual Encounters)

by

Brendan Hawthorne

Set in a virtual museum, Exhibit B explores facets of memory and fantasy and how remnants of those memories can be illuminating or disorientating to our well-being as they are inputted and stored upon a hard drive of sub-consciousness.

It is written through the eyes of a seeker visiting influential halls of mirrors displayed on screen in temporary exhibition rooms before they are deleted or given a permanent space by the omni-present guide.

Exhibit B

I

Snow falls in penny-flake fan-tails
Driven on
within whirlwind hornet-hives
their collective history is sent swirling
into a tumult of reflections
news-flashed
and mashed
in the diesel-grime hub-cap mirrors of
brushed-lacquered steel

On
and on

they are sent scurrying
from the tracks and along
faceless footfall avenues
towards neo-gothic relay stations
and the brittle columns of
communications devices
whose only purpose is to
relentlessly transmit sound bytes
to anyone who's receiving

I didn't see what happened to each

of the individualised
crystallised forms
once they had filed past me

Neither do I care

Up until now I've never been too interested in creation theories
or the perception of their chaotic
collective exchanges
However
I am now suddenly aware of my physicality
and personal space
as
vulcanised pneumatics shhh my soapbox thoughts
into silence
and indolence

For a split second I feel akin to those aluminium air-stream bullets
the ones with tow-bar extensions
I watch them migrate along
hardcore routes
promoting their
'hook-seeks-eye'
nature and purpose
their articulated union manufactured in a state
of inter-dependency

a need born of momentary principle

One

by one

they slip away with my connections

transporting telegraphed fragments

of ideology

to far flung destinations
evening flaring around them in trails of
red, amber and white
Each moment of reckless fantasy
is seized upon and forced
to take its place at the next halt sign
or alternatively
launch themselves into an eccentric orbit
around a terra-firmed traffic island
where they are left to find happiness in the company of strangers
and witness freedom sinking into the ashes of confinement
In the distance a stereo-type
screams for forgiveness
its cry quickened in the beat
of heart-beat
pulse-beat
reflex-driven bass-beats
cannoned from parcel shelves

violating the relative silence built up
within neuron-riven cavities
Gorged by ergonomically designed
ear-pieces
they independently tell a half story
In tandem they preserve the isolation
of a city street
seemingly bereft of values

No-one was giving way

And the forecast?

Grey

II

The building I had been seeking
lurchsd forward
Pushing its way to the front of the queue
revealing itself from the pasty background of a typically inner-city
crass-morass skyline
Its entrance
is of a resplendent
neo-classical form
and thankfully not that of a flamboyantly fickle mock baroque
dictate
A serpentine marble stair
as cold as a grave
sweeps from the arc of a semi-automatic
half-glazed honey-oak door
I am ushered in by tradition
I am drawn impulsively towards
the wrought iron banister
that corrals a tightly bound
spiral staircase
as it curls its way
smoke-like
ever-upwards to a point
that seemingly
could lie on the leading edge of infinity

In stark contrast
CCTV eyes roll
They invade space and liberty
each scene viewed via the encased sockets
of polished glass
focusing on all actions and thoughts
before being recorded and sent through processing servers
a continuous monitoring policy
for individual safety
and training purposes
whilst the
echoes of distant voices patiently cling to the magnolia as they wait at the
ticketed turnstile
Witnesses observe the soft sheen paint as it soothes the skin of skimmed
plastered walls
which restrain the tension of boiling brickwork now buckling under a
restless and resistive conscience

Ascending the stairs to a mezzanine floor
all movements are sound-tracked by jazz
a freeform ooze
café blue
hemp-bloom blown on Pan horns
left smouldering
at the back-door gates of hell
its melody lost in a raging torrent
of hardcore hard-drive rumble

YOU ARE HERE

III

A post-menstrual blond with faded glamour
steps out from the half-light
and welcomes me to this mausoleum
of recognised thoughts
deeds and illusions
Each one in turn has to be
registered

logged

and

inventoried

before becoming

sterilised

homogenised

and

sanitised

Bagged

tagged

and readied

for easy consumption

She remembers how to purr seduction

by singing lullabies to my nightmares
clutching me to her bosom
and guiding me blindly along the tiles
She advises me not to
step on the cracks for fear of forfeit
and informs me
a little too casually
that she can talk to the dead

Her words hold a cold
callous
eye-of-the-storm conviction

A stone-carved mind
now duly magnetised
is relaying an
unwanted message to bore at my emotions
a worm programmed to gorge
on pulp fat

Her eyes shine
They are roadside cats eyes
giving me the go ahead
She hands over a transient's guide book
presumptuously marked with
what she feels

is an interesting route for me to take
through the exhibition halls
Each corner is crammed with
attic tea chests
that have become washed up
and left strewn along gutters
and alleyways
only to be preserved
in dusty back rooms
on tea break guilt trips
They are
dis-jointed
reminders
of how things used to be
She freely offers me
the courtesy of a sickle moon smile
I ease my way past her
Contact is unavoidable
She blushes with the intensity of a black rose
and bleeds........

IV

A gunshot rings out
It might be a news story
or a starting pistol
It's time to go
Anonymous footsteps
drum the stone stairs as
I make my way along corridors of culpability
apathy and desire
My path is marked in red
and I notice that the entrance door to the
first exhibit has been re-varnished
several times
yet remains wedged-tight
in its frame
A brass handle turns with worn-loose ease before the room yields
to personal insistence

Overhead
an oval sign reads........

The

Sunflower

Lounge

The room is dour and smells of emissions
stale liquour and strong body odour

Barfly belches
Sits on
Two-tone stool
Dralon maybe
Sucks vermouth
Into dry mouth
He's way too cool
To turn around
Instead draws on
Ice and bitter lemon
Mops lips
With padded wipe
And snaps
Ginger fingers
Orders again
This time absinthe
He ignites
Opiate-laced narcotics
At the touch
Of a micro-switch
Draws smoke
Across clenched teeth
And exhales

Hisses plumes of
Azure
A ghost
Sits quietly in the corner
Flashes gold teeth
Tips the scales
And weighs
Moonshine
Against
Sunshine
Before panning
A profit
A string quartet is
Wrapping up Bartok
As the jukebox
Hits Bird
Outside
Darkness fans neon
And consumes
The essence
Of innocence
Laid immeasurably
And consistently
At the feet of
Midnight terror
I walk to the bar

I am given a drink
It's my usual
I sit back
On the block sofa
Partially hidden
By parlour palms
So that I can
Knock-back space
And time
I wait for a text
From someone
Interesting
Nothing arrives
I observe
A drunk
Who's getting forcibly ejected
Over an unpaid bill

I am left
Lost
And
Within a single measure
The dream ends........................

But the hallucinations begin at 3.15am

V

The clock always reads 3.15
it's accusing gnarled fingers
pointing
directing and demanding
that I take notice
The bar is closed
I am on the outside looking in
Only emergency exit lights guide me back
to an earlier point of entry
The door is locked and without handles
I'm being refused access to numbness
and my mind is becoming
a raging bush-fire
I take a deep breath in
It fans the flames
to furnace intensity

In my heart I am freezing

Along arterial red routes
crystal-ice flurries burn
They are corrosive amber suns
setting along
sodium-stream boulevards

The sky explodes as comets fry ozone
in the tense atmosphere
sparking up the onset
of a chain reaction fever
an eruption of ego
blaring along a corridor of corruption
found running through the darkest recesses
of my soul

Across city quadrants
steel grille shutters
blank out weary eyes
from window shopping

Botticellian women
are sent to
check out recently acquired
baubles to hang off
the fuller figure
in the privacy of their own
fantasy rooms
before peering
into wide-screen
LCD street-wides
stretched across
xenon fizz corners

hung up
on wall-to-wall asphalt
where Elvis meets Marilyn
Passionately he kisses
her red-bow lips between
monochrome flickers
as he feels his way
gently around the curves
Time is running out
for the hour-glass figure
and the freeze-frame
gets locked away
preserved forever
all wrapped up in a final take
Hollywood cellophane
bound over
to keep it's peace
in the cocooned security
of carefree sensuality as
slab sluts pick their way
through ram-raid shards
and ride high on snapped-off stilettos
their systems
fuelled on trans fats
and re-tread re-bores
They sing to a familiar tune as

M.C.'s spit bars
in a sound check
bin-lined bass box
Across the skyline
of broken teeth
and sagging clouds
wailing sirens
mourn cold reality
to the heat of the night

VI

The subsequent reference point
directs me towards another exhibit
I reach the door
knock
and wait
before entering

Through the glass I see abstraction
Wall-mounted abstraction
set in jagged jangles of angular projections
Noisy colours roaring through repression
Their black bevelled frames restraining them like rabid beasts
they long to break out
and
leap from the nails that stretch the canvas in taught precision
They are prison panels
of violence and degradation
ignorance and hardship
Places where freedom can be devoured before age can decay
They have become sheets of colour candy
ready for easy use
and personal pleasure
Fauvism always reminds me of
Fruit Spangles

beach holidays and summer specials
but……
always
always
always
with abstraction
I have to wrap myself up for winter
to find some semblance of contentment

Chasing swarm shadows from multiple
spot lamps
I see cross-fade
as I eclipse them
Denying light to a darkened microcosm
I enter the space with tense and paranoid uncertainty
just as the artist
a featureless man
brushes past me to leave
He moves in the same way that he paints
sometimes directionless and without goal
sometimes obsessed with expression
anger and violence
He attacks the innocence of canvas
stabbing the paint
into each raised follicle
Hue by hue

he reduces emptiness
into a single statement
that comes to life
through oil and paint
swirling on the palette
rotating in
fingerprint whorls of recognition
each image electrifying with charged intentions
some dampened in linseed
others accelerated by terpentine

They cry out!
Each and everyone of them
cries out!
An experiment
in sound and vision
Tint and tone
link arms in
processions of light
and ignite
incandescently arranging
Harmonising rage
with peace
A juxtaposition
of references
pushes me

to the edge
It beckons me
to surrender
and succumb
to the inner self
now desperate
to find itself
in an atmosphere of self-imposed
incarceration
I am left to seek justice
from experience
and to find solace
within turmoil

A bell-phone rings in the distance
No-one gets it
Optimistically I follow its bright peal
only to find it screwed to a graffiti wall
in a tumble-weed dust-ball
backroom
It is a mind-space canyon
resounding the vibe
all plumped up letters
and blown-out cartoons
heroes speaking in bubbles
and advertising riddles

Talk is cheap but
words are charged for by the minute
I lift the receiver with a degree of hesitancy
and a cold voice devoid of feeling
whispers
It's not over yet
A dialling tone is left to punctuate
before
silence shouts out
that it desperately seeks company

VII

Sitting on a common-space bench I look down onto the street
below
through a low andnarrow window
An old man
bleached with cold and age
stamps his feet
on a street corner
counts out time
He is sawing through a violin
to keep warm
He smiles at the pennies
as they fall into his cup
like tears
Towards the reception area
a wall-mounted television is broadcasting snow in high definition
It is sequenced to the sound of
white-noise static
Above
the sun is boiling cloud-forms as they scurry from the base-line
horizon
The arc of Venus reclines and

reflects on her conjunction with the solar phallus that has just
ejaculated the seeds of dawn

into an unfilled promise

And in the comfort of a vacant doorway

A shadow
shakes change
through beggared pockets
His eyes are fixed
to a dark point
in his memory
as he stands behind
the pretty chick who's
trailing perfume
fresh from the shower
The taint of
last night's indulgences
sours his breath
He got off before his stop
and smiles at her
like a reptile
as she passes him by
In his heart they are lovers
In his mind's eye
he has had her
and she hates him
for it
but he doesn't know why

An alarm wails
Snaps at synapses like a mad dog
baring down on brittle bones
It's on-time and time to move on

The next door is blind
No windows
No key
and no handle

I run my finger around the sealed edge
I draw splinters and expose tears in the flesh
The door springs open
seemingly of its own volition

'ENTRE!'

is shouted from the guttural depths of
a gravel-voiced female
I shuffle my leaden feet into a palace that breeds dark enterprise
passion
and delusion
A woman with leather skin
lies draped in spun-silk throws
that lie shot with barbs
She is garishly illuminated by

floodlights
They are halogen-hot and
as cold as tungsten
Her laced-up waist is cinched
and topped
by a cupped-hand whale-bone
A blue light shadow-crimps revealed flesh so that it resembles
ripples on water
Gemstone-blue rock pools
shimmer as
dusky segments of areola rise above the harsh edge of the
saloon-girl basque
Opalescent stockings encase her legs with the colour and
iridescence of peacock feathers or that of a changeling's wings
It's really hard to tell

She bends forward
accentuates her hips with soft-line
elegant fingers
her spaghetti strap underwear
clearly disappearing under the honesty of
micro-weave lycra
She lifts the mini hemline
and moves with feline balance and prowess

I have become indecisive and blush like a chameleon on a

vermillion sheet
A small satin triangle obscures her liberty as she walks mercurially
across the floor to the door of a cupboard marked

'DANGEREUSE'

The words are written in red cellulose or maybe blood
Each letter in turn leans to the right and is jagged and angular in
execution

I am transfixed by longing and loss that reside in my captive eyes
as they

feast upon the image

now presented in half-light snatches

She approaches

carrying a carpet-bag that bears a name on a dog-eared
buff luggage tag
She has my measure and I
reassuringly
think I have hers

She orders submission
She says she likes to watch
a man's blood blister
through his sweat
as it simmers to the surface
in an eruption of carnal energy

She remains
unfeeling and momentary
just as my recklessness
dissolves into melancholy

Wrapped up
Bound up
Beaten and
gagged
Submissive Oppressive
meets
Dominant Suppressive
and
desire locks away the heart
with
a key
last seen
in post-coital
ambience
loaded indifference
fear and dread
A b-bomber babe
gets caught up
in a see-through wrap
She cleans up her act
Says she has

another date
and time
to deal with
and files it away
intact
Her soul is
wearing thin as
she shows another man
the door
Wipes lipstick
from his jaw
and leaves him
naked
to his public
dressed only
in a flush
of guilt
and effusing the
unmistakeable stench
of stale musk
now leaking
from every pore
of his oily
saline skin

Outside

traffic crawls into hibernation
Engines are running
but are disengaged
left to idle and
offer no torque
Along road networks
empty office complexes
face up to the reality
of commercial plug-ins
their crumbling façades
supported by
scaffolding and
triangulated box crane jibs
a collection of tangents
and signs
considering each move
as red eye beacons
look out as far
as the crane flies

DANGEREUSE

VIII

Elsewhere snow cleans dirt from broken streets
as Joe and Josephine Public blow blue-mist trumpets into the thick
snow dome atmosphere
weighing up will and grinding down time to a beleaguered doldrums standstill

Guilt-ridden and satiated I feel a sense of amusement breaking out across my face as I reach the next door

My teeth are dry and snag on cracked lips forming a snarl in the mirror
The skin on my back stings
with whale and nail marks
Like a couch of nettles they remind me of her and the cruelty that lies in her mind
and within her sex
I hear the flytrap snare snap its jaws
across the hall as
another victim is claimed
another specimen
ready for the page

Next door laughter is heard
I cross the threshold

into a busy room
A lead-filled ragtime piano stops in mid bar as though an axe has cleaved
the crotchet in two
Once inside I find
animated flick books
They flik-flak stories
at a pace
indexed to
the nimbleness of finger and eye
Comic space westerns depicting six-shooter space-ray outbursts run
with an unconvinced audience
They are films on fire
Their outbursts
warping the magnetic heads from reel to
take-up spool
Their projections traversing angles as an accusatory commentary
prognosticates on the validity of celluloid when reaching out to
infiltrate the masses

Another example of corporate desire is destined to leave the consumer with
over-exposure and consumption hangovers
An explosive cocktail mixed with passion finds history in reach
even though it's as out of step as the hand-crank projectionist
trying to match the wrist action of an artful camera-man

Images are crystal
Hard edged black-and-white
No room for colour in these frames

Above airships are nudging each other against a grey
gull-back sky
Gantry tethers anchor-encased pressure
in dome-fin envelopes
Their demeanour and shape sagging like
storm clouds before the bluebirds can sing again from
suspended cages
A record is playing a big band sound
We jitterbug
my followers and I

We wait in shadowy reflections for your grand but long overdue
entrance

Between the drapes
Silver nitrate
Explodes into stars
Household names
Cascade from
Living room to

Kitchen sink
Urban jungle to
Outer space
Reaching out
Across the projectionist's
Inverted beams
Of industry
Multi-media is
Shaping
Moulding
Leading
Fashion
Philosophy
And propaganda
A new regime
Hidden in
The schmaltz
A big time
Winner
In the small print
And the names
Of those
Who never made it
Are sent falling by
The wayside
Into ditches

Marked Despair
Drunkenness
And
Obscurity
Who measures
Their lost potential?
Their input?
Their scene change?
They fall
From grace
Consumed by
A dark lunar tide
Their faces ageing
In real time
Not preserved
In the can
Down the lane
All washed-up
In a headline
Found drowned
In a spirit bottle
Another genius
Free from contract
and fear of
Contradiction

In the distance an ice cream van chimes summer
I run towards it....
I hear childhood
and witness
its departure
I'm sorry
I dropped the cone
At the cemetery gates

Ice cream!
Ice cream!
Get your ice cream!
Nice ice cream
Ice cream
Ice scream
Ice scream

I scream!
An usherette with a candy pink smile and blue starched hat
escorts a battery light
ice-tray with a logo that looks like a
chrome-winged cruiser

A film slip-slaps in abandonment from an upstairs room
The last show is about to commence once the audience is seated
and a new feature is found

I look into the piercing eyes of a lady with a
frost burn tan
She sits alluringly in a front row plush velvet armchair
I see that she is crying
She tells me
-between sobs-
that her screen hero died dramatically
in the penultimate scene of the last spool
She waited for hours at the bus stop and
there was a sunset waiting for them to ride off int
but he didn't show
No romance or sustainability
She said he was prone to over-acting anyway and asks if I would
love her tonight
The usherette winks and blows a kiss as she adjusts her
foundation wear
and lights a cigarello
held loosely between her
moist cherry flesh lips
Her smoke curls
ever upwards
A helicoil staircase
cushions the cosmos
I want to draw in her exhalations
Taste her once more
Hi-fidelity holds me back

roars a theme tune as

I leave with the tip-seat charmer clinging to my arm as the

house lights dim down on the lonely

We kiss in the half-light

It was more comfortable there
We could share our demons
in armchair seats
set on the brink of ecstasy
before the next act
but somehow we knew
that we needed to break away from
the hunting pack of media chasers

IX

We remain
tingling in the afterglow
of a stand-up quickie
Other strangers remain fused
on a common thoroughfare
seeking a moment of comfort
somewhere along a corridor marked
'Trickery'

The clock said 3.15
It always did.........

Its gothic fingers spread like
the welcoming arms
of a gnarled tree

A door
left ajar
beckons me towards flashing lights and the promise of a payout
I am breathless
panting hard
my temples pulsing with engorged blood trying to break through
the road-block
and access the by-pass freeway to
another town

I'm waiting to implode

My head swims in misty vertigo just before the floor rises up

hits my face full on with a pass out to a pipe organ fade-out finale

I come to in a panic

just as rocket ride carousels threaten the moon with invasion but

it'll never come off

Always too much gravity keeping them anchored to good old

Blighty soil

A man sits with his arm across the sofa

He flicks channels on a closed circuit TV

He swims in white noise

and drowns in the shallow end

The titles fade out and a new scene begins

You really are a miserable bastard!

He already knew that one

A shining example

of a considered observation

delivered with force

just as he was about to make

the killer move

and go for a home run

Every woman he had been close to

had said the same thing

He always worried about letting
down the guard
always better to let down lovers
than the all-important guard
So he was left alone again
with the sound of a slamming door
punctuating her last statement
with enough finality
to chill the cold even further
that ran through his veins
chased by rye to exorcise
his low spirits
His eyes wept
staining the busy
evening rush hour
of headlights and tail lights
that wound restlessly
around the streets
he overlooked from the
fourth floor rented apartment
The evening colours ran
into a stained glass patchwork
that hypnotised and soothed
his lurching emotions
He needed a voice
someone to be kind to him

He dialled out for a pizza to share
listened to a bright
accepting voice
that took his orders
so he thought to ask
what time she finished
and if she'd come
and deliver
personally

Drawn by arcade lights and amusements

I sigh with familiarity as a one-armed bandit spins fruit bowls in its gap-toothed smile

its hollow chest rattling with payout convulsions
coughing up a free-play promise
for the price of a hold
and a nudge

I need air but there is no way out
All the signs read
Way In

The joystick crane offers the last grasp hope of a free pass out to one lucky winner

The prizes seem guarded
The wrapped-up fiver and the green dinosaur
try to remain anonymous
An unlucky portent for the loser
I use the free-play that's now
burning a hole in my pocket
I have thirty seconds to prove myself
My reflexes are slow
An uncertain hand
misses salvation by a fraction
forcing me to make do with a mystery card

There is panic in my reflection as Venetian blinds cut swathes
across the tile floor in horizontal slashes

They are the bar code price of freedom
but I have nothing
left in my soul
to barter with
I scan the room

A bluesman sits in the corner with a trilby hat
at his feet
he cradles a guitar
like a newly born babe

He lights up and sings

I have holes in my shoes
Can't pay my dues
I'm a real low downer
With one careless owner
The only thing that I can sing
Is the blues
I've been known to confuse
When bearing old news
I'm a real low downer
With one careless owner
And the only thing that I can sing
Is the blues
I've got some personal views
I'm prone to effuse
'cause
I'm a real low downer
With one careless owner
And the only thing that I can sing
Is the blues
I walk in the rain
No-one to share my shame
I lose each of my friends
Like they're fashion trends
And the only thing
That I have left

Is the blues

X

I catch the smell of sea air as I walk along an
open stairwell
It has the familiar scent of brine and sea kelp
I remember a story
through newspaper clippings
It was a funny business.......
Everyone interviewed said that
he died with the call of a clown
wedged silently in his mouth
his body found lifeless and face down
on a rock-strewn beach
An offshore wind
sifted sand through
a technicolour wig
he had bought second-hand
from a hire shop window
He saw the world
through a kaleidoscope
He even thought he could fly
from a cliff top launch pad
Unfortunately he met the ground too fast
and much too early
He'd overstretched himself
Committed himself to ridicule

In the boozer Henty
recalls him being a jellyfish of a man
No wonder he was all washed-up
in the end
Tugger Pip Evans
threw down a rope
cursed the man who kept him
from his teatime rum
and bitten briar pipe
as he winched aloft
the curlicue form
and saluted it aboard
on the screaming cables
of two-stroke cradle arms
The Stoneguard Watch
Chisel-faced Dolan
weeps for his lost love
as he realises he was still owed
a massive fifty quid
Out across the wind chime forest
of harboured masts
port lights and starboard home
they all set sail to the inns
to the rap
of pedestal glasses
drumming like fools

as they

damn the dead of night

and an old tune runs through my head

XI

A thaw takes hold on neighbouring rooftops causing ice to fall in rafts

onto the

momentarily deserted

street

Tiny rivers flow

into debris cluttered gutters where innocence lays its sweet head
on sullied pavements and waits for the good grace of a kind Samaritan

I am reminded that salvation comes in

empty glasses

There's a bar twenty-four seven
on Baltimore Street
There's a bar twenty-four seven
on Baltimore Street
There's a bar twenty-four seven
on Baltimore Street
It's been driven into disrepair
hastened by traders in white powder
and hasty plastic pen pushers
who seek to revamp the urban form
between their close-knit communities
Outside a neon sign with

a cracked tube traces the words
No parties
Prior booking
is essential
You have to order
a good time here
Take it whilst it's going
or miss the boat
because
beyond the perimeter fence
marine ply
protects shot glass windows
and bill posters will definitely
be prosecuted
In the highest courthouse in Christendom
on the junction with Hope
a man of few words prays
for deliverance and apologises
for seeing things so quietly
His road has met the sky
a million miles too late
turning his shoes into sandals
on the way to promised lands
He says God I prayed
God I prayed
God how I prayed

I prayed every single step of the way
with my eyes closed and
I missed the journey of deliverance
I missed the journey of deliverance
I missed the journey of deliverance
My eyes were shut tight
as tight as clenched fists
and I missed the journey of deliverance
Picking up the pieces is so much easier
hunched over with a heavy heart
than forgetting it all in a moment
I prayed every step of the way and
I missed the journey of deliverance
I missed the journey of deliverance
until salvation dropped in
Told me to give out toy phones
to anyone passing by
with a card that read
'Ring treble zero'
Connect with yourself for free
or tune in to the recorded wisdom
of the street evangelist
He's always engaged in that good book
Look him up
Leave a message
Wait for an answer

whilst big business buffs its nails
and signs another deal
over lunch
You see greed always delivers
Next day satisfaction guaranteed
It helped me towards the darkness
Helped me towards the darkness
Helped me towards my darkness
Finger-posting my options
when I stood at the crossroads
and cried out for help
I spun that empty spirit bottle
and woke up in the sanatorium
with a demon at my side
You see the devil comes to you
He cares about the pay off
not you
He cares about himself
not you
He cares about
his bonus cheque on Judgement Day
as another lost soul
leaves a message for the Samaritan
to place in order of need
because if there was no more suffering
there would be no more need

If there was no more war
there would be no more need
If there was no more starvation
there would be no more need
If there was love in this world
there would be no more need
and
I missed the journey of deliverance
because I wanted the destination so bad
and I hadn't got a heart-felt ticket
for Christ's 'Happy in Heaven' bus tour
I felt they'd all been taken long ago
and my pilgrimage was on blistered feet
and hunger
not first class on the gravy boat
And all I have is what I stand in
All I have is what I stand for
and all I have are scars
that remind me of the wounds
All I have is this street corner
and your vague indifference
What do I know?
And all I have are these six strings
And all I have are these ideals
I missed the journey of deliverance
because I had my eyes closed

as tightly as a fist
And all I have left is this street corner
and a mind that's free to choose
Help me
Help me
Help me
in this moment of desperation
as the sun sets
so deeply in the west
I need to believe!
I need deliverance!
Salvation!
But where are they kept?

XII

A new opening appears in front of me
It has sought me out
and gives me no choice
but to confront it
head-on

A dull metallic thud sickens the air as I lift the hand-beaten latch to enter
The door screeches on rust lined hinges and slams-to behind me leaving me in partial darkness
A presence guards two candles that glimmer in the void
like firebrands cooling into winter heat
Each is sentinel to two further doors
I am compelled to make my choice before I'm paralysed by darkness
I close my eyes
and enter another dimension
The door slams shut and bolts are drawn like sleepers across the boards
I am not alone
My eyes flutter in REM mode sending out a Morse Code distress signal
for anyone to receive
The room is devoid of air

Stale
hot and humid
each pore of my skin swells noisily
Walls seem keen to meet on mutual neutral territory and make
their way to where

I think I stand

I am lost and disorientated
I hear fan blades cutting the atmosphere into time periods but I
cannot find myself whichever way I count or stack them

A shadow casts disturbance
A blown kiss on the cheek is scented with
palma-rosa
She is with me
an angel of light
A torch-bearer resident
in an open mind
Funny
I remember that father was a scorpion
He'd strike out at the full-faced full moon as it peaked from behind
the chiffon clouds that lay strewn across a battlefield sky

The remnants even now cloud my vision

I am a fish
Waiting to rise from the depths of a
murky incarceration
I am waiting for the tide to turn my way

Get the upper hand as I wait
The luminous fingers on the clock state
3.15 am
It is always 3.15
An alarm clock rings in the distance and I recall that I was only ever happy in dreams until now

A cool hand
Reaches out
To a cold heart
Palpates it
And breathes life
In a pulse beat
The ailing
Atmosphere
Dispels will
Yet
She walks
Amongst us
Treads the
Twisted nap
Of an unfinished
Tapestry
And in one breath
Inflates lungs
From shallow

Flutterings
And
Follows fate
Whose trick hand
Allowed
This life to
Turn blindly into a
Cul-de-sac

I awake
A hard stained pine bench cold rivets my spine against its surface
The wood smells of age and solvent abuse
and so do I

A stained glass sunrise greets sleep-filled nightmares as they
scurry away to hide

In carp-mouth recesses

They are but phantoms kissing the coat-tails of night-visions

sent screaming away to die in sulphurous light filters

The fever has gone and the atmosphere is as cool as a forest floor
I breathe again
Above
the skylight frames freedom
as birds air their wings
tipping their flight to the edges of space in preparation for

migration
I am not of their world
yet
their nature is of mine

A cuckoo in the nest whistles on the hour
as the techno-preacher begins the next lesson

Praise be to the desk-slave multiplex
altar to the world-wide-web of intrigue
and home to the sacrificial rites of duplication
Meditate and salutate to this
the filtered rising sun
of hood-winked Sodom street lamps
and be liberated of the feelings of reverse paranoia
that betrays the faces of the accusers

I'm gathered in
a Lepidoptera lured to a striking match
set like a jewel in a shop front portico
depicting social retail theory
and the effects of advertising
A flute is blown
and an acoustic drum
beats the bounds of change

Barefoot meditations
bleed over the crystal jags
of imported lager bottles
Closed eyes
connect senses
to the scent of
moss-coated lime bark
transpiring profusely
Biding its time for
moonlit alleyways
and linear groves
to draw the traveller in
along its smooth sides
seducing the soul
into reaching out
to find the warmth
of another
and share the intimacy and
vulnerability of a park bench
feeling the contours
between the legs
to the tender ridge
and witnessing
the blushing onrush
of tears

Beyond the bridge
lies a jetty
dedicated
to the rich
and the exploited
as they stand in lines
shoulder to shoulder
locked forever
in a war on ethics
The accusatory finger
of a worshipful steeple
grey with age
turns towards those who've
lost their way
and have encountered
themselves in the blind alleys
of forgotten paths
and lost ideals
before inviting
their nightmares home
to take tea with mother

XIII

A room cries out with
the deeds of a bitch
on Hell's heat
Caught up in headlight overcoats
her lips are polished as red as
fire extinguisher sentinels
She sends out alarm signals
setting them off one-by-one
in speculative releases
They arc their pressurised content across
free-space rainbows that
reward tension with freedom
At a distance hotel banners
rip through the twilight
Their proximity eats away at the horizon
by replacing artistic vistas with pre-formed
concrete sound bites
deliberately designed to exhaust reddened commuter eyes still
further
as leather uppers and man made soles
pace along spit-stained castellated streets

A kiss at the gates
of coffee and fag breaks

adds intrigue to the monotony
of a crow-hammer sunset and the vision
of a woman dressed in poncho and trainers
Her crumpled crazed lips
punctured by too many arrows
speak through rollers
roll-ups and ring pulls
She begs for a few pounds more
just to see her through the impending night
of obsession and fear
so that she can caress her demons
suckle them on her dry breasts
and consume them all in one last lick
of a dry tongue over a crackle-glaze opening
She steadies herself for another day
to break over the heads of fools

Another door beckons

My curiosity out-weighs my fear and I knock assuredly before removing the barrier and crossing the threshold

A train whistle blows in the distance and carbolic coke and steam invade the echoing hallways of my memory

How we would laugh when we ran from the brass scales with a quarter of satin purses swagged away in a paper cone

Everyone would look old

and we felt so young

We never thought our turn would come when we were gobbing off the

Great Western railway bridge

straight into the funnels of passing loco's

We had soot in our lungs and smoke in our eyes

We were Jack-the-lads
pretending to pull a drag from
chocolate cigarettes
And there we were
accompanied by
Jill-the-wenches swapping gobstoppers
sitting on the garden wall of Miss Jenkins
until we were all swept along by a bristle brush
a hard stare and a waving fist

The girls would giggle and call her an old tart because the story was that when Miss Jenkins worked at

The Miners Rest Public House

she would spit in the bull's eye beer mugs and wipe her lipstick round the rim with a glass cloth They said she smiled as she did it because she'd never been close to a man but many a man would have tasted her lips

XIV

I focus on a room
A man is sitting at a walnut desk leafing through pages of images
Some of them are hand cut in black and white others are machine guillotined and are in colour

An anglepoise lamp with
Arthritic hinges
Sparks up and
Is directed towards me
Points an accusing
Artificial sun deep
Into my starry eyes

He pauses
Holds the abscess on his hand and swears it will be the death of him
The pages continue to turn
I am bound up with familiarity
The images I recognise
They are of me

Outside

sleet falls in laser darts

piercing the armour of overcoats

and brightly coloured shower-proof over-jackets with absolute precision

People bob along gutters in fluorescent waterproofs

like fishing floats

Dragged on currents
Going with the flow
Every so often
one will try to forge its own way
before finding
it was just the long way around
The collective skin flexing and tingling
in hive recognition

I am transported to caravan holidays and summer rain

The sea boiling like lead

I recall how the only brightness was looking at the sky through the amber roof vent or listening to the popping gas mantle that illuminated the fold-down card table in the bottle gas glow of an asbestos filament

The simplest soup tasted so good from the lip of a crazed steaming mug as overhead arguments peppered silence with the bluntness and persistence of artillery fire

I kept my head down then
It is no different now

There is movement as
The shadow man sits in a halo of silence
Turning the pages
Of an old album
He appears unmoved
Patterns!
He shouts
All patterns!
We all follow patterns
We need them sometimes
And sometimes we don't
We crave for what we desire
What we can't have
Spend a lifetime in trying to create an ideal
When all along we screw up
Miss opportunities
Throw them to the floor
Unwanted cast-offs
Laid to waste
And they would have led us there
We need to see the way
not just long for the destination
That will arrive in due course
Look at me
Look deep into my eyes

Into my soul and who do you see?
His eyes are emotional torrents
forming light spangles on still waters
I see the beginning
And the end
I see myself
And all who have gone before
And what is to come of it?
I cry
All the poison
All the bitterness
All the frustration
Pain and hurt is cleansed
and transformed
into butterflies
that find open windows
and colour them with life
Staining them
with perfection
I watch them air their wings
and find a way out
and migrate towards
fresh hope

The gallery is closing
Last admissions only

I'm offered an evaluation sheet
There's an empty space
for a forthcoming attraction
No takers
just rumours

Walking through the honey-oak
exit doors
I turn my back on winter
and enter
a vernal equinox
The guide smiles a sickle moon smile
waves
sighs
and bleeds
blushing as I ease past her
to find my own elements

The guide book is taken from me
and is torn to shreds
by her manicured hands
its composition thrown high across
the glistening rooftops
Each of the pieces fall like snow
The script is broken into phrases

Scattered remnants destined for the street below
Some drift softly into doorways
and get left behind
Others gather pace and intensity
and are
blown along in penny-flake fan-tails
Driven on
within whirlwind hornet-hives
sent scurrying
along gutters
as the clock releases its tension
moves a reluctant gothic finger
on an out breath
and points to
3.16

XV

PAY ATTENTION!

Another minute of
another lifetime
is about to be broadcast
on loop
It may be yours
Scheduled and exhibited
It will be labelled for recognition purposes
before being stifled in an environmentally controlled vault
Occasionally it will be inspected for conformity
Is there anyone receiving?
This warning message is about to be ....

DELETED

www.ingramcontent.com/pod-product-compliance
Ingram Content Group UK Ltd.
Pitfield, Milton Keynes, MK11 3LW, UK
UKHW020236250726
13967UKWH00001B/405